CLEVELAND CAVALIERS

ALL-TIME GREATS

BY TED COLEMAN

Book design by Jake Slavik
Cover design by Jake Slavik

Photographs ©: Ron Schwane/AP Images, cover (top), 1 (top), 12, 21; Frank Gunn/The Canadian Press /AP Images, cover (bottom), 1 (bottom); Focus On Sport/Getty Images Sport/ Getty Images, 4; Mark Duncan/AP Images, 7, 8, 10, 14, 18; Mark J. Terrill/AP Images, 16

Press Box Books, an imprint of Press Room Editions.

ISBN
978-1-63494-601-8 (library bound)
978-1-63494-619-3 (paperback)
978-1-63494-637-7 (epub)
978-1-63494-653-7 (hosted ebook)

Library of Congress Control Number: 2022913240

Distributed by North Star Editions, Inc.
2297 Waters Drive
Mendota Heights, MN 55120
www.northstareditions.com

Printed in the United States of America
Mankato, MN
012023

ABOUT THE AUTHOR

Ted Coleman is a freelance sportswriter and children's book author who lives in Louisville, Kentucky, with his trusty Affenpinscher, Chloe.

TABLE OF CONTENTS

CAVALIERS
34
CARR
34

CHAPTER 1

FIRST WINNERS

The Cleveland Cavaliers joined the NBA in 1970. Their first seasons did not include much winning. But players like **Bobby "Bingo" Smith** helped change that.

Smith was a master of long jump shots. The swingman was also reliable. In nine full seasons he never missed more than 10 games.

Austin Carr became known simply as "Mr. Cavalier." The guard averaged more than 21 points per game as a rookie. Carr sometimes battled injuries in his career. But he was healthy in 1975–76. That helped the Cavs make their first playoff run.

The center on that team was **Nate Thurmond**. Thurmond was at the end of a legendary career. But the 6'11" big man brought defensive toughness to the Cavs.

Brad Daugherty followed as the Cavs' next great center. The team selected him first overall in the 1986 draft. He played his entire career in Cleveland. He was an All-Star in five of them.

THE MIRACLE AT RICHFIELD

The Cavaliers made the playoffs for the first time in 1976. They opened with a tough opponent. The Washington Bullets had three future Hall of Famers. But the Cavs pushed the series to seven games. Game 7 was at home at Richfield Coliseum. The Cavs' Dick Snyder made a shot to remember. His 12-foot jump shot won the game and sealed the series. The "Miracle at Richfield" is still a proud moment in team history.

CAVS
43
PAXSON
CAVS
DAUGHERTY
43

Daugherty helped lead another era of playoff basketball in the late 1980s.

The 6'11" **John "Hot Rod" Williams** formed a strong duo with Daugherty. Williams grabbed a lot of rebounds and scored a lot of points from under the basket. He also found success as the team's first man off the bench. Running the offense was **Mark Price** at point guard. Price created points with both his passing and shooting.

Larry Nance flew into Cleveland as a former Slam Dunk Contest champ. But it was his defense that made the difference for the Cavs. Nance became one of the best shot blockers in team history. The three-time All-Star helped lead the Cavs to the 1992 conference finals. This era is still beloved by Cavs fans.

STAT SPOTLIGHT

BLOCKS IN A SEASON

CAVALIERS TEAM RECORD

Larry Nance: 243 (1991-92)

JAMES
23
SPALDING

CHAPTER 2
KING JAMES

Center **Zydrunas Ilgauskas** came to the Cavs in 1996. He proved to be a great rebounder and inside scorer. But the Cavs rarely made the playoffs. In 2002–03, they managed to win just 17 games.

However, all that losing earned them the top draft pick. They used it to select forward **LeBron James**. Cleveland fans already knew James. He was born and raised not far away in Akron, Ohio.

Basketball fans everywhere knew all about James, too. He was one of the most promising

VAREJAO
17

STAT SPOTLIGHT

POINTS PER GAME IN A SEASON

CAVALIERS TEAM RECORD

LeBron James: 31.4 (2005-06)

young players ever. James lived up to that in winning Rookie of the Year in 2003–04. And that was only the start.

Ilgauskas developed into an All-Star. He and James formed a "big three" with forward **Drew Gooden**. Gooden and Ilgauskas were strong rebounders. Gooden also could score under the hoop.

Gooden had arrived in a 2004 trade. That trade also brought in **Anderson Varejao**. The big man was a force under the basket. He made life tough on opponents trying to score.

His energy and effort made him a favorite among fans.

These players formed an important supporting cast for James. "King James" turned into one of the greatest players ever.

He could play anywhere on the floor. His passing, shooting, and defense were all among the best in the league. Behind James, the Cavs reached their first NBA Finals in 2007.

In the 2008–09 season, **Mo Williams** came to Cleveland in a trade. The point guard took over running the Cavs offense. He soon had to do it without James, though. James left for the Miami Heat in 2010. Williams stepped up as team leader. It was up to him and Varejao to keep the Cavs competitive.

COACH BROWN

The Cavs hired Mike Brown as head coach in 2005. The 35-year-old was the second-youngest coach in the NBA. But he proved he was ready. In just a few years he led the Cavs to 66 wins. He was the fourth-youngest coach in league history to win 60 games. Brown never had a losing record in his first five years as head coach.

IRVING
2
CLEVELAND
SPALDING

CHAPTER 3
FINALLY CHAMPS

Replacing LeBron James was impossible. But winning the first pick in the 2011 draft certainly helped. The Cavs chose point guard **Kyrie Irving**. Irving was a skilled playmaker. He was an even better scorer. He averaged more than 20 points per game four times in Cleveland.

Cleveland also held the fourth pick in 2011. The Cavs used that on **Tristan Thompson**. The big man soon proved to be an elite rebounder.

However, these players could not get the team back in the playoffs. Then one big signing changed everything. James returned to Cleveland in the summer of 2014. Fans had been hurt when he left in 2010. But they were thrilled to see him again.

A trade later that summer also brought **Kevin Love** to the team. Love was an elite rebounder. He could also score from both the inside and outside.

The Cavs were transformed. They returned to the NBA Finals in James's first season back. Guard **J. R. Smith** was another reason why. Smith brought energy and attitude to the team. He was also a great shooter. That helped as the team made a run back to the NBA Finals in 2016. This time James finished the job. The Cavs won Cleveland's first major sports championship in 52 years.

STAT SPOTLIGHT

CAREER POINTS

CAVALIERS TEAM RECORD

LeBron James: 23,119

The Cavs made two more Finals with James but lost each. James then signed with the Los Angeles Lakers. This time the rebuild went better. Cleveland used a high draft pick in 2019 on point guard **Darius Garland**. Garland was an explosive scorer who could shoot threes.

Center **Evan Mobley** gave the Cavs a presence under the basket. Mobley had the skills of a guard at 7' tall. The combo of stats he put up was unusual for a big man. There was only one LeBron. But fans hoped the Cavs now had the players to win a title without him.

FATHER AND SON

Uniform No. 22 is retired in Cleveland. It belonged to Larry Nance from 1988 to 1994. But the team made an exception. Larry Nance Jr. arrived in a 2018 trade. He was the son of the Cavs legend. Nance Jr. played four seasons in Cleveland before being traded in 2021.

WESTFIELD
CAVS
4
CLE
MUNITY
MOBLEY
4

TIMELINE

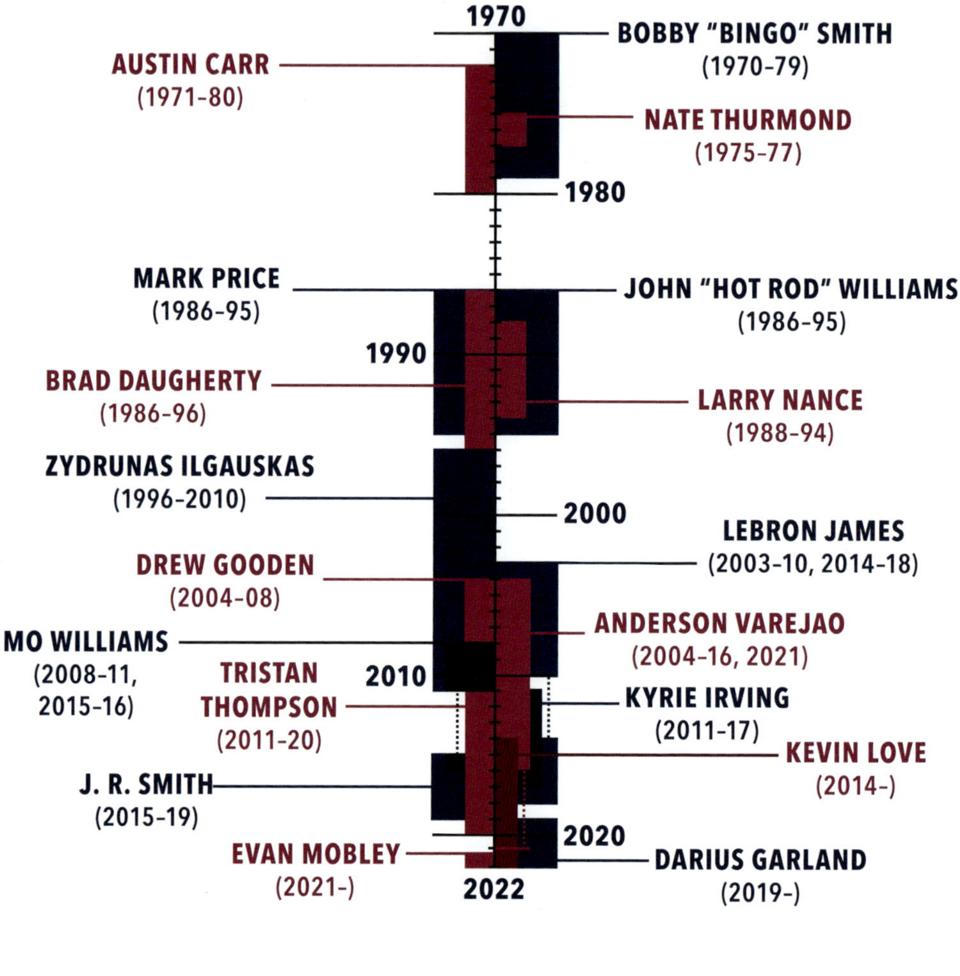
1970
BOBBY "BINGO" SMITH
(1970-79)
AUSTIN CARR
(1971-80)
NATE THURMOND
(1975-77)
1980
MARK PRICE
(1986-95)
JOHN "HOT ROD" WILLIAMS
(1986-95)
1990
BRAD DAUGHERTY
(1986-96)
LARRY NANCE
(1988-94)
ZYDRUNAS ILGAUSKAS
(1996-2010)
2000
LEBRON JAMES
(2003-10, 2014-18)
DREW GOODEN
(2004-08)
ANDERSON VAREJAO
(2004-16, 2021)
MO WILLIAMS
(2008-11,
2015-16)
TRISTAN
THOMPSON
(2011-20)
2010
KYRIE IRVING
(2011-17)
KEVIN LOVE
(2014-)
J. R. SMITH
(2015-19)
2020
EVAN MOBLEY
(2021-)
2022
DARIUS GARLAND
(2019-)

TEAM FACTS

CLEVELAND CAVALIERS

First season: 1970–71

NBA championships: 1 (2016)*

Key coaches:

Mike Brown (2005–06 to 2009–10, 2013–14)
305–187, 42–29 playoffs

Tyronn Lue (2016 to 2018)
128–83, 41–20 playoffs, 1 NBA title

MORE INFORMATION

To learn more about the Cleveland Cavaliers, go to **pressboxbooks.com/AllAccess.**

These links are routinely monitored and updated to provide the most current information available.

Through 2021–22 season

GLOSSARY

conference
A subset of teams within a sports league.

draft
A system that allows teams to acquire new players coming into a league.

elite
The best of the best.

playoffs
A set of games to decide a league's champion.

rookie
A first-year player.

swingman
A player who can play both guard and forward.

INDEX